THIS BOOK BELONGS TO:

✳

....

· ·

🐕

"No man fails who sets an example of high courage, of unbroken resolution, of unshrinking endurance."

– Roald Amundsen

Dedicated to Nick Grill

Special thanks to Judy Grill, Kit Grill
Mike Atkinson, Alex du Cros, Harry Tennant, Chris Haslam,
Mina Bach, Dan Lockwood, Sam Arthur, Alex Spiro
Lee Glasspool and Sue Clark.

SHACKLETON'S JOURNEY

William Grill

FLYING EYE BOOKS

LONDON ✳ NEW YORK

CONTENTS

INTRODUCTION
1

FUNDING AND RECRUITMENT
3

THE CREW
5

THE DOGS
7

ENDURANCE
9

EQUIPMENT AND SUPPLIES
11

SETTING SAIL
13

FROM ENGLAND TO SOUTH GEORGIA
15

EXPEDITION MAP
17

INTO THE WEDDELL SEA
19

PACK ICE
21

ENDURANCE STUCK
23

A CHANGE OF PLANS
25

WINTER MONTHS
27

ISOLATION
29

PRESSURE
31

ENDURANCE LOST
33

OCEAN CAMP
35

THE MARCH
37

PATIENCE CAMP
39

ESCAPING THE ICE
41

SAILING TO ELEPHANT ISLAND
43

ELEPHANT ISLAND
45

PREPARING THE JAMES CAIRD
47

SAILING TO SOUTH GEORGIA
49

MEANWHILE ON ELEPHANT ISLAND
51

MAP OF SOUTH GEORGIA
53

CROSSING SOUTH GEORGIA
55

STROMNESS WHALING STATION
57

RESCUE
59

DEPARTURE
61

THE ROSS SEA PARTY
63

HOME AT LAST
65

GLOSSARY
67

INTRODUCTION

Born on 15 February 1874, Shackleton was the second of ten children. From a young age, Shackleton complained about teachers, but he had a keen interest in books, especially poetry – years later, on expeditions, he would read to his crew to lift their spirits. Always restless, the young Ernest left school at 16 to go to sea. After working his way up the ranks, he told his friends, "I think I can do something better, I want to make a name for myself."

Shackleton was a member of Captain Scott's famous Discovery expedition (1901-1904), and told reporters that he had always been "strangely drawn to the mysterious south" and that unexplored parts of the world "held a strong fascination for me from my earliest memories".

Once Amundsen reached the **South Pole** ahead of Scott, Shackleton realised that there was only one great challenge left. He wrote: "The first crossing of the Antarctic continent, from sea to sea, via the Pole, apart from its historic value, will be a journey of great scientific importance."

On 8 August 1914, Ernest Shackleton and his brave crew set out to cross the vast south polar continent, **Antarctica**. Shackleton's epic journey would be the last expedition of the Heroic Age of Antarctic Exploration (1888-1914). His story is one fraught with unimaginable peril, adventure and, above all, endurance.

FUNDING AND RECRUITMENT

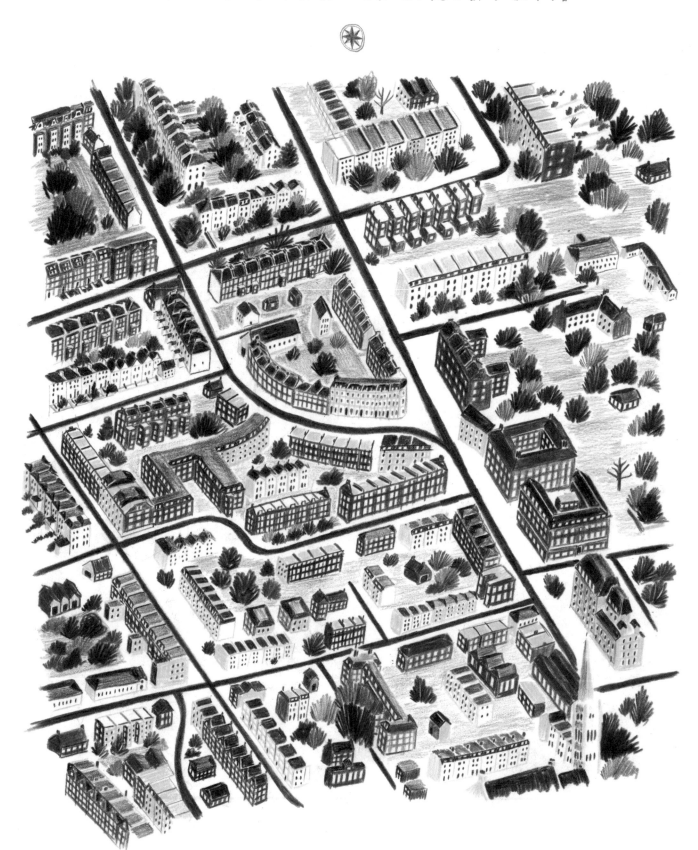

The Shackletons had moved house many times, from Athy in County
Kildare, Ireland to Yorkshire to London. Just before Shackleton left
for Antarctica again in 1914, he lived in Kensington, West London.

Shackleton's first challenge was to raise enough money to support the expedition, and this proved very difficult. However, after much effort he was able to secure the thousands of pounds he needed. Life boats were named after the sponsors – the James Caird, the Dudley Docker and the Stancomb Wills.

During the recruitment process, Shackleton quizzed candidates on their practical skills, but also about more unusual things, like if they could sing well. Second-in-command Frank Wild helped Shackleton to choose 26 men from the 5,000 that applied.

THE CREW

FRANK WORSLEY
Ship's captain.

ERNEST SHACKLETON
Expedition leader.

FRANK WILD
Second-in-command.

LEONARD HUSSEY
Expedition meteorologist.

GEORGE MARSTON
Expedition artist.

WALTER HOW
Able seaman.

REGINALD JAMES
Expedition physicist.

THOMAS ORDE-LEES
Motor expert and storekeeper.

JOHN VINCENT
Boatswain and able seaman.

TOM CREAN
Second officer.

WILLIAM STEPHENSON
Fireman and stoker.

ROBERT CLARK
Expedition biologist.

JAMES WORDIE
Expedition geologist.

TIMOTHY McCARTHY
Able seaman.

ALFRED CHEETHAM
Third officer.

FRANK HURLEY
Expedition photographer.

DR. JAMES McILROY
Second surgeon.

DR. ALEXANDER MACKLIN
Expedition surgeon.

LIONEL GREENSTREET
First officer.

ERNEST HOLNESS
Able seaman and stoker.

HUBERHT HUDSON
Navigating officer.

CHARLES GREEN
Ship's cook.

ALEXANDER KERR
Second engineer.

LOUIS RICKINSON
Chief engineer.

THOMAS McLEOD
Able seaman.

HENRY McNEISH
Ship's carpenter.

**WILLIAM BAKEWELL
PERCY BLACKBORROW**
Able seaman. Stowaway.

THE DOGS

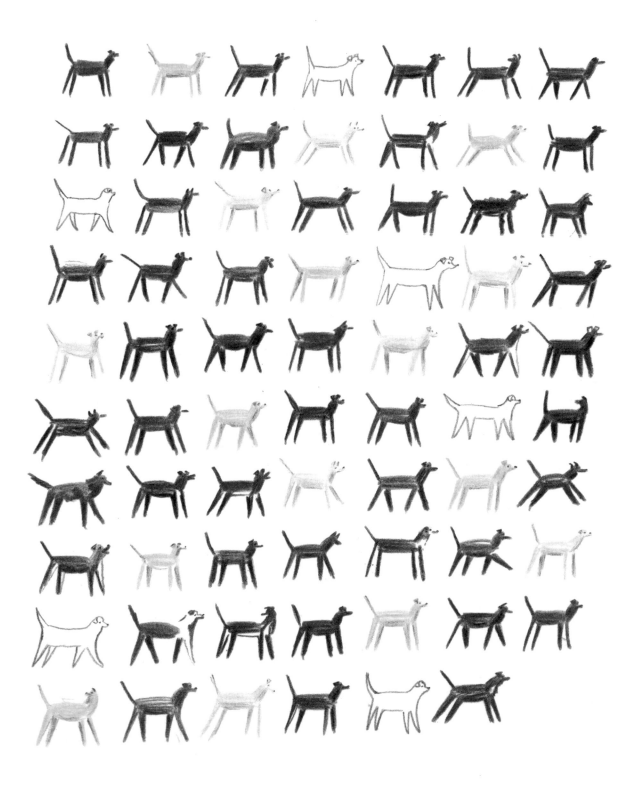

In 1914, a cargo of 99 dogs was sent from Canada to London. Of these, 69 were chosen for the expedition. Shackleton and the crew gave them all names, and you may notice that some are named after famous people and crew members.

The dogs came from a mongrel mixture of breeds, including Newfoundlands, St. Bernards, Eskimo dogs, Wolfhounds and wolves. Cross-breeding the dogs meant that they were very strong and had qualities such as a thick coat or a good temperament. The average weight of each dog was 100 lbs!

They included:

Alti, Amundsen, Blackie, Bob, Bo'sun, Bristol, Brownie, Buller, Bummer, Caruso, Chips, Dismal, Elliott, Fluff, Gruss, Hackenschmidt, Hercules, Jamie, Jasper, Jerry, Judge, Luke, Lupoid, Mack, Martin, Mercury, Noel, Paddy, Peter, Rodger, Roy, Rufus, Rugby, Sadie, Sailor, Saint, Sally, Sammy, Samson, Sandy, Satan, Shakespeare, Side Lights, Simian, Slippery Neck, Slobbers, Snowball, Soldier, Songster, Sooty, Spider, Split Up, Spotty, Steamer, Steward, Stumps, Sub, Sue, Surly, Swanker, Sweep, Tim, Upton, Wallaby, Wolf.

The lively dogs were to play a vital role in Shackleton's expedition. Their ability to pull more than their weight, brave the cold and work in packs meant that they were at home in Antarctic conditions. They were expected to cover up to 20 miles a day with a loaded **sledge**.

Each crew member was assigned at least one dog to care for, and many developed strong bonds with them, especially second-in-command Frank Wild, Tom Crean and the photographer Frank Hurley.

ENDURANCE

Originally intended for tourist cruises and polar hunting, the Endurance (or Polaris as she was initially named) was perhaps the strongest wooden vessel in the world with the exception of the Fram. She was named Endurance after Shackleton's family motto: *By Endurance We Conquer*.

Endurance was designed by Ole Aanderud Larsen, and constructed under the watch of master shipbuilder Christian Jacobsen in Framnaes shipyard in Sandefjord, Norway.

Jacobsen, being a meticulous craftsman, made sure that all the men who worked on the ship's construction were experienced seafarers as well as skilled shipwrights.

One of the main differences between the Endurance and the Fram was that the Fram was bowl-bottomed, allowing her to rise out of the ice if she became stuck.

Luckily for Shackleton, the original owners Adrien de Gerlache and Lars Chistensen were in financial straits and desperate to sell the ship. Being supportive of Shackleton's intentions, they were happy to sell the ship for £11,600 (approx £45,000 in today's currency), a fraction of the original cost.

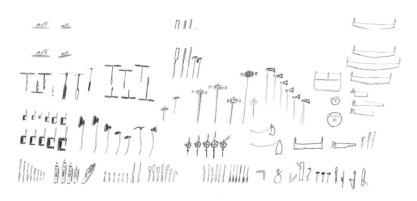

Being such a unique ship, Endurance had to be worked on with a whole host of conventional and unconventional carpentry tools.

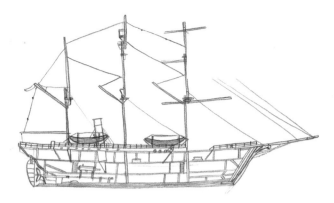

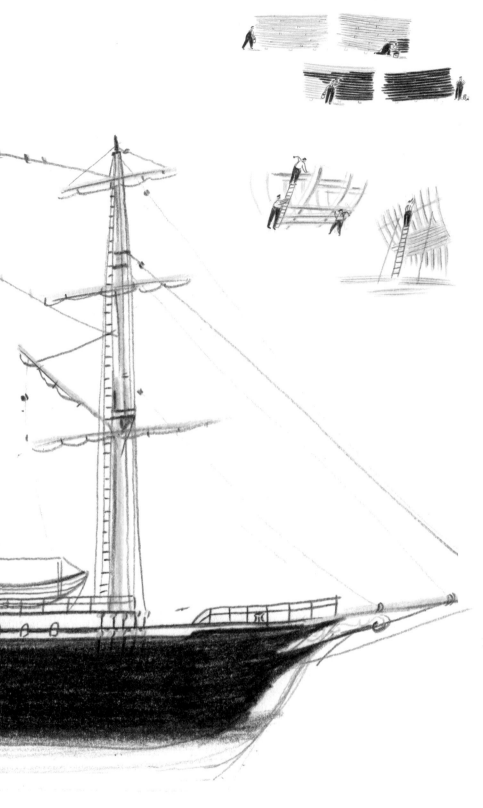

A very robust and sturdy little ship, Endurance was designed specifically to withstand harsh polar conditions. This meant that wherever possible joints and fittings were **cross-braced** and strengthened, making her extremely strong.

Later on, a platform was rigged under the **jib boom** so that Hurley was able to film the ship breaking through **pack ice**.

The bow (the front) would be used like a battering ram to break up thick ice, so it had to be especially strong. In total, it was 1.3 metres thick!

Endurance was built from Norwegian fir, oak and greenheart.

Her keel was made up of 4 sandwiched pieces of solid oak, totalling to a thickness of nearly 2.2 metres, while both her sides were 0.7 metres thick.

Each piece of timber had been selected carefully from a single oak tree, so that it would fit the design and curvature of the ship.

EQUIPMENT AND SUPPLIES

As well as supporting a crew of 28 men and 69 dogs, Endurance carried a large amount of cargo. Journeying into the heart of Antarctica meant that Shackleton would need to carry a whole array of exploration equipment and supplies to keep him and his crew alive in hostile conditions, from sledges and skis to blankets and mitts.

Just before departure, Shackleton was presented with the Union flag by King George V, who encouraged him to bring it back safely.

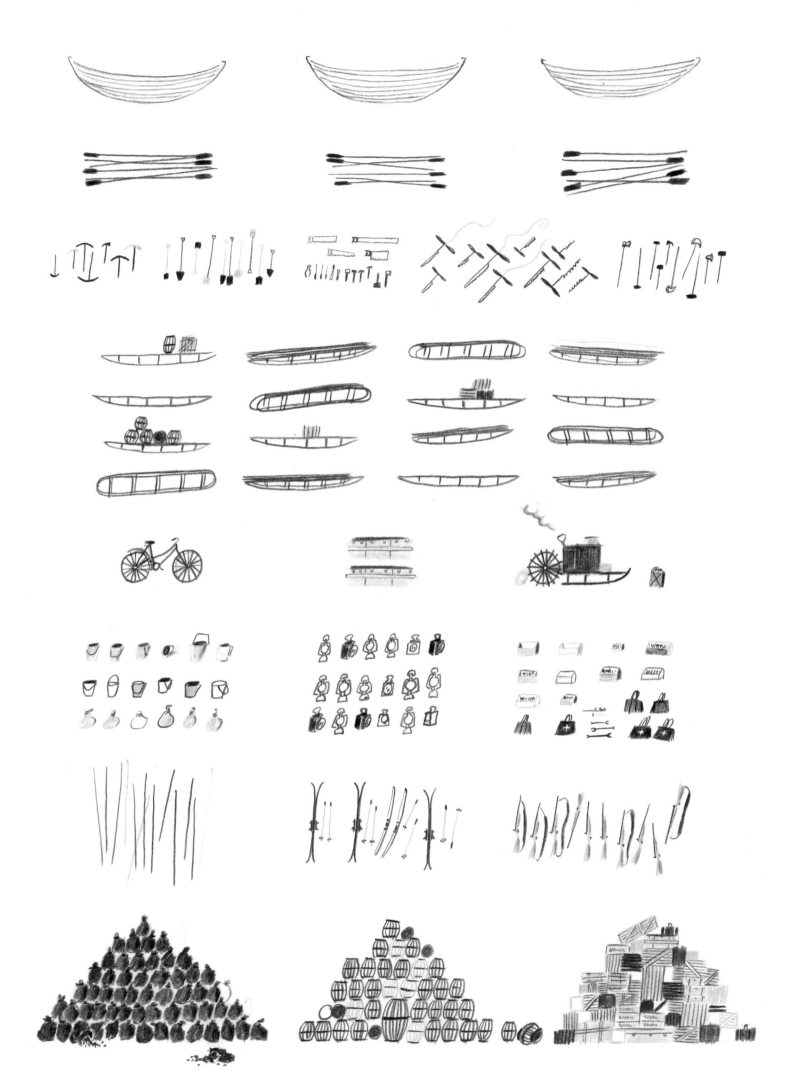

SETTING SAIL

✳

Endurance set sail for Buenos Aires on Saturday, 8 August 1914, after receiving a telegram from the Admiralty which simply read, "Proceed".

FROM ENGLAND TO SOUTH GEORGIA

The journey from Plymouth to Buenos Aires was fairly uneventful. However, a few crew members were dropped due to drunkenness and insubordination. Luckily, the experienced Canadian seaman William Bakewell joined the crew, as did a plucky 19-year-old stowaway, Percy Blackborrow.

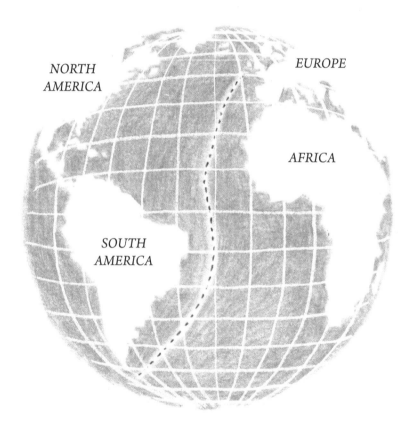

The crew then spent a month making final preparations at Grytviken whaling station, the southernmost outpost of the British Empire.

Ready at last, the ship left South Georgia on 5 December 1914 and headed for the South Sandwich Islands.

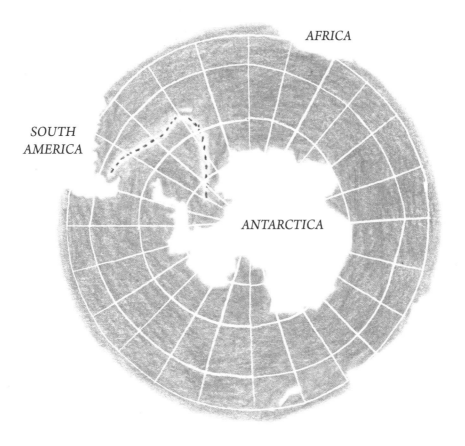

AFRICA

SOUTH
AMERICA

ANTARCTICA

In Shackleton's words, "The long days of preparation were over and the adventure lay ahead."

EXPEDITION MAP

ATLANTIC OCEAN

SOUTH AMERICA

ELEPHANT ISLAND

LIFEBOATS SET SAIL

PACIFIC OCEAN

ENDURANCE LOST

ENDURANCE BESET

ELLSWORTH LAND

PENSACOLA MOUNTAINS

TRANS-ANTARCTIC RIDGE

THE SOUTH POLE

SOUTH GEORGIA

SEA

DENSE
PACK

LOOSE
PACK

ICE
SHELF

INDIAN OCEAN

SØR
RONDANE
MOUNTAINS

ANTARCTICA

QUEEN
FABIOLA
MOUNTAINS

INTO THE WEDDELL SEA

Soon after entering the Weddell Sea, Endurance began to encounter pack ice, which resembled something close to a giant jigsaw puzzle of ice stretching for over 700 miles ahead of the ship.

Occasionally the **foresail** was **reefed** so that dangerous **growlers** might be spotted and avoided. Shackleton was fond of **conning** and working from the **crow's nest**, as he could see for miles. Animal life was abundant here, and included crab-eater seals, humpback whales, ringed penguins and many other seabirds.

PACK ICE

Progress was slow and laborious. Of the 700-odd miles of pack ice, the last 250 miles consisted of tough, solid ice up to 3 feet thick, with pieces up to a mile long. The ship would repeatedly ram the ice at half speed to weaken it and carve a V into the ice edge. Then the ship would fire its engines and drive full speed into the ice like a giant wedge. Hurley filmed this process while hanging below the jib boom.

Initial contact with the pack ice was exciting, but it soon became something of a concern as the ice became thicker and tighter. Endurance had to work harder and harder to break through.

ENDURANCE STUCK

Finally, after battling bravely through over 700 miles of pack ice, Endurance was overcome. As far as the eye could see, she was surrounded.

After waiting ten days, Shackleton ordered the fires to be put out in order to conserve fuel. Before attempting to break free, he waited for conditions to improve. During this time, there was an opportunity to test the motor sled, and the men had time to relax.

On 14 February, Shackleton ordered a good head of steam, and Endurance creaked and groaned as she tried to free herself from the cruel grip of the ice. For over 48 hours, the whole crew attacked the ice furiously with ice-chisels, picks and saws. The little ship eventually moved, although it was soon beset again – 400 yards of heavy ice lay between her and open water.

Exhausted and beaten, all the crew could do now was wait.

A CHANGE OF PLANS

Shackleton briefed the men on a new course of action: Endurance would now become their winter base. Hoping that spring would bring better fortune, he planned to keep the men busy, training the dogs and preparing for the ice to break up. But how far would they drift before that day came?

Dog **igloos** were built out on the ice, made from wood and snow. Overjoyed to be off the ship, the animals soon settled into 'Dog Town'. McNeish constructed a stove, which became a popular spot for the crew to hang out. At the same time, the inside of the ship was remodelled to improve life on board. The new living quarters, always bustling with activity, were known as the Ritz.

The dogs were divided into teams, and training continued over several months. Pulling sledges and learning to work together, the dogs and the crew quickly became firm friends. Apart from the training, the crew had plenty of things to keep them active. Whenever possible, they would try to catch penguins to increase their food stocks, and the constant build-up of ice on the ship needed to be removed at regular intervals. Stores were also reorganised in case they needed to be removed from the ship quickly.

WINTER MONTHS

The crew passed the time fishing, hunting penguins and taking scientific measurements. Vibrations and **pressure ridges** in the ice meant that the men had to be extremely careful when they were out on the **floe**.

As May and June went by, the expedition passed into twilight and long, dark days lit only by the moon.

Meanwhile, the dog teams began holding races. In June, the crew held an Antarctic derby, with Frank Wild snatching an exciting victory over Frank Hurley.

Despite the pressures of leadership, Shackleton knew it was vital to keep the crew's morale high. On Midwinter's Day (21 June), the crew celebrated with speeches, songs, toasts and a rousing rendition of the national anthem.

A severe **blizzard** a few weeks later saw winds of between 60 and 90 miles an hour, and Dog Town was buried under 5 feet of snow.

Finally, in early July, the sun began to return.

As the ice floe continued to buckle, provisions were made for emergency evacuation of the ship. New **kennels** were built on the upper deck, and tensions mounted as the pressure around the Endurance continued to grind ice against the **hull**. Soon after, loud cracks were heard from the ice as pressure forced huge blocks up into the air, and the dogs were hurried back onto the ship.

ISOLATION

Endurance was now 500 miles from the nearest civilisation…

PRESSURE

Another roaring blizzard heaved the ice into a maze of **hummocks**, and as the pressure around the ship continued to grow, the crew realised they might have to escape at any minute.

Intense pressure on all sides began to push the ship up out of the water. By October, Endurance was tilted at a 30-degree angle, and still the ice showed no mercy.

Finally, the ship began to crack as it was twisted out of shape. A loud bang was heard and water flooded in. Luckily, McNeish managed to fix the dangerous leak, but conditions continued to worsen.

With pressure ridges rising all around them, Shackleton reviewed his plans to evacuate the ship, which was being crushed from all directions.

The force of millions of tons of ice made it too perilous to stay onboard. As the ice roared deafeningly, the men were ordered off Endurance and onto the ice.

They set up a temporary camp where they would be safe from harm, and a new plan of action could be made.

Endurance creaked and groaned as the strain increased, and loud cracks and deafening sounds were heard as the ice slowly crushed the cross-bracing of the ship.

Frank Worsley wrote, "The behaviour of our ship in the ice has been magnificent... It will be sad if such a brave little craft should be finally crushed in the remorseless, slowly strangling grip of the Weddell pack, after ten months of the bravest and most gallant fight ever put up by a ship."

Despite such grim circumstances, Shackleton remained positive in front of his crew. "So now we'll go home," he remarked calmly. A new challenge rested on his shoulders: their mission now was to survive.

ENDURANCE LOST

"We were helpless intruders in a strange world," Shackleton wrote, "our lives dependent upon the play of grim elementary forces that made a mock of our puny efforts."

And then it came. On 27 October, the brave ship that had struggled so far was now crushed beyond hope of repair. Endurance sank a little, her deck breaking up gradually, and then water began to pour in. The state of Endurance left all the crew heartbroken. She had battled 1,500 miles of ice only to meet this sad fate.

OCEAN CAMP

Ocean Camp would be the crew's new home for the next two months. Each morning, dog teams set out under Frank Wild's supervision to salvage boats, sledges, **rations**, fuel and equipment from the wreckage of Endurance. She finally sank on 21 November 1915. Having left South Georgia almost a year before, the crew was now drifting helplessly on an ice floe at the mercy of the wind. They hoped to drift north into the open Weddell Sea, from where they could sail to land. With warmer weather approaching, the ice was beginning to weaken and could break up at any moment. Always diligent, Shackleton made sure the camp could be packed up in just five minutes.

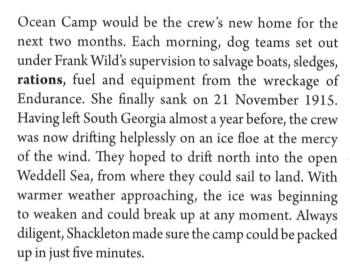

Life on the ice was not altogether bad, though. Time was spent hunting, reading, repairing kit, drying clothes and making weather observations and navigational readings. Meanwhile, Shackleton worked hard to provide a varied diet for his men so that their morale was kept high. He did this by combining tinned provisions with seal and penguin meat. Hurley created a **blubber** stove, and food became central to keeping up good spirits. Yet, despite their attempts to stay cheerful, the men were eager to be on the move.

THE MARCH

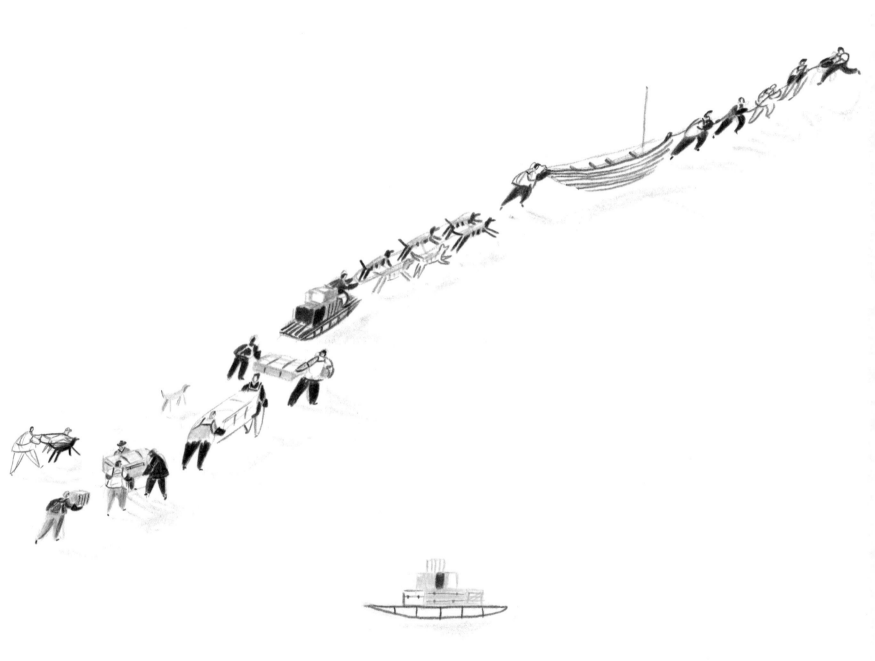

On 23 December, Shackleton and his men packed their remaining possessions and left Ocean Camp in search of safer ice. It was a long march. Exhausted and weakened, the crew and dogs worked heroically, pulling heavily loaded sledges for seven days and seven nights.

PATIENCE CAMP

Patience Camp would be the crew's new base for the next three and a half months. Time passed slowly. Parties were sent out daily in search of seals and penguins, because rations were now running low. A cooking igloo was constructed for Green, and he did extremely well in the tight conditions. The other men spent the time reading from the Encyclopaedia Britannica and testing each other. However, the camp was not without its problems. Contrary to Shackleton's wishes, Orde-Lees would go on solo ski hunts in search of food. Shackleton needed to ensure the safety of all his crew, so ordered Worsley to keep an eye on him.

Even though supplies were low, Shackleton made an effort to celebrate the leap year, giving the men a boost they all needed. Out of nowhere, a ferocious **sea leopard** ambushed one of the men, but luckily Wild was on hand with his trusty rifle. Upon preparing the animal for cooking, they found that the belly of the beast was full of undigested fish!

Due to the rapidly worsening condition of the men, and the drifting of the ice floe, Shackleton made plans to head for land in the boats. Sadly this meant that the few remaining dogs had to be shot, as there would be neither food nor space for them onboard.

ESCAPING THE ICE

After six months on the ice, Shackleton and his men were now balancing precariously on a raft of ice that was beginning to break up. They had to move.

Sailing was dangerous, as fast, foamy water hurled blocks of ice to and fro, while waves cast 60-foot sprays of icy cold water.

As light faded, camp was pitched on a large, flat floe. That very night, the ice split and Holness fell into the dark water. Luckily, Shackleton was nearby to rescue him.

Shackleton and Wild captained the James Caird, Worsley directed the Dudley Docker, and Hudson and Crean were in charge of the Stancomb Wills.

But the three boats had to push on as far as they could. Their lives depended on reaching land as their supplies were now limited by the size of the boats.

When Shackleton asked if Holness was alright, he replied, "Yes, Boss, only thing I'm thinking about is my baccy (tobacco) I'd left in the bag."

After taking refuge in their boats and having little sleep, the crew set out again at 6 am, heading west. They stopped early, having been at the oars for over 36 hours.

But the men were never out of harm's way. As they huddled in their boats, killer whales surfaced nearby, hissing and splashing, and almost **capsizing** them.

Despite the bitter days and nights, Wild remained as cheery as ever, steering the boat on towards the warm prospect of breakfast.

As the smoke and smells rose from the little stove, the men's hearts were lifted. The cook's abilities were truly tested on treacherous rafts of ice.

Progress was slow, and Shackleton now decided to tether the boats together for security. The Stancomb Wills had to be towed by the James Caird, as she could not keep up.

Exhausted, the men clung together for warmth as snow fell silently, covering them like a white blanket. The struggle for survival was taking its toll.

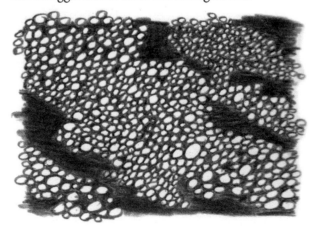

SAILING TO ELEPHANT ISLAND

✳

Given their current position and condition, Shackleton now decided to make a dash for Elephant Island, 100 miles away. Worsley navigated well under the harsh conditions, using only a pocket **compass**. After over 108 hours of toil, the men were exhausted, frozen like statues, their hands crooked around their oars. **Frostbite** was now affecting the whole crew. But the sight of dry land was electrifying. Soon they would be the first men ever to set foot on Elephant Island.

After 16 long months, the crew had found solid ground. Dehydrated and hungry, each man ate and drank until he was full. But their troubles were not over yet, as the coastline was exposed to the elements, and a cruel blizzard set in for days…

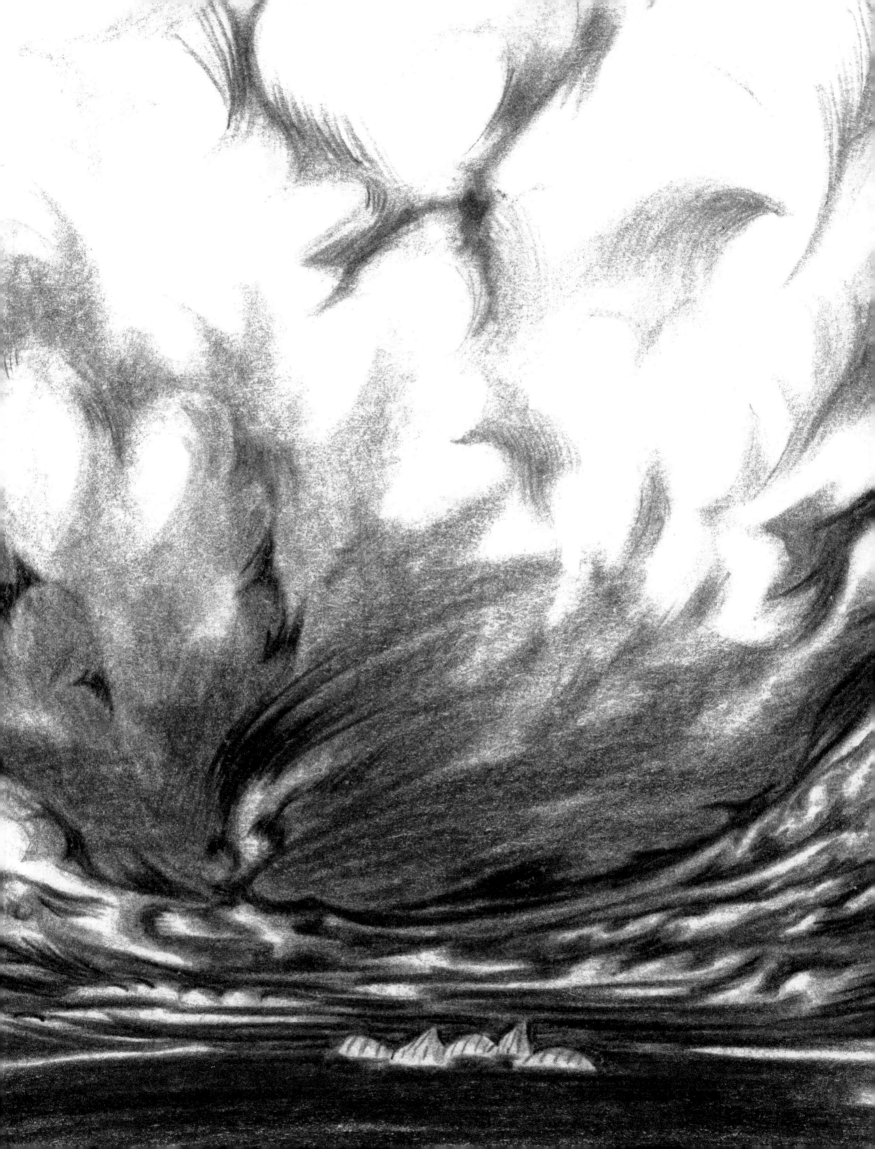

PREPARING THE JAMES CAIRD

The condition of the crew was now deteriorating further; they had been surviving on scanty means for over 16 months. Since no ships pass Elephant Island, Shackleton decided they must sail to South Georgia to seek help – a journey of over 800 miles.

He discussed his plans with Wild and Worsley, and decided he would take one boat with a small crew, leaving Wild behind to look after the rest of the men. McNeish the carpenter strengthened and refurbished the James Caird ahead of the voyage.

This would be an extremely hazardous journey. The ocean south of Cape Horn was perhaps the most treacherous in the world, known for its deadly **gales**.

McNeish, McCarthy, Vincent, Worsley and Crean were chosen to accompany Shackleton on his epic journey to South Georgia.

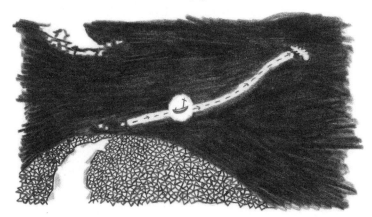

Enough provisions for six months were taken:

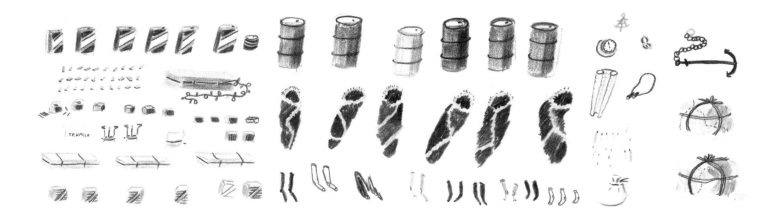

As the little boat moved away, the group on the beach gave three big cheers, and watched as their friends disappeared over the horizon.

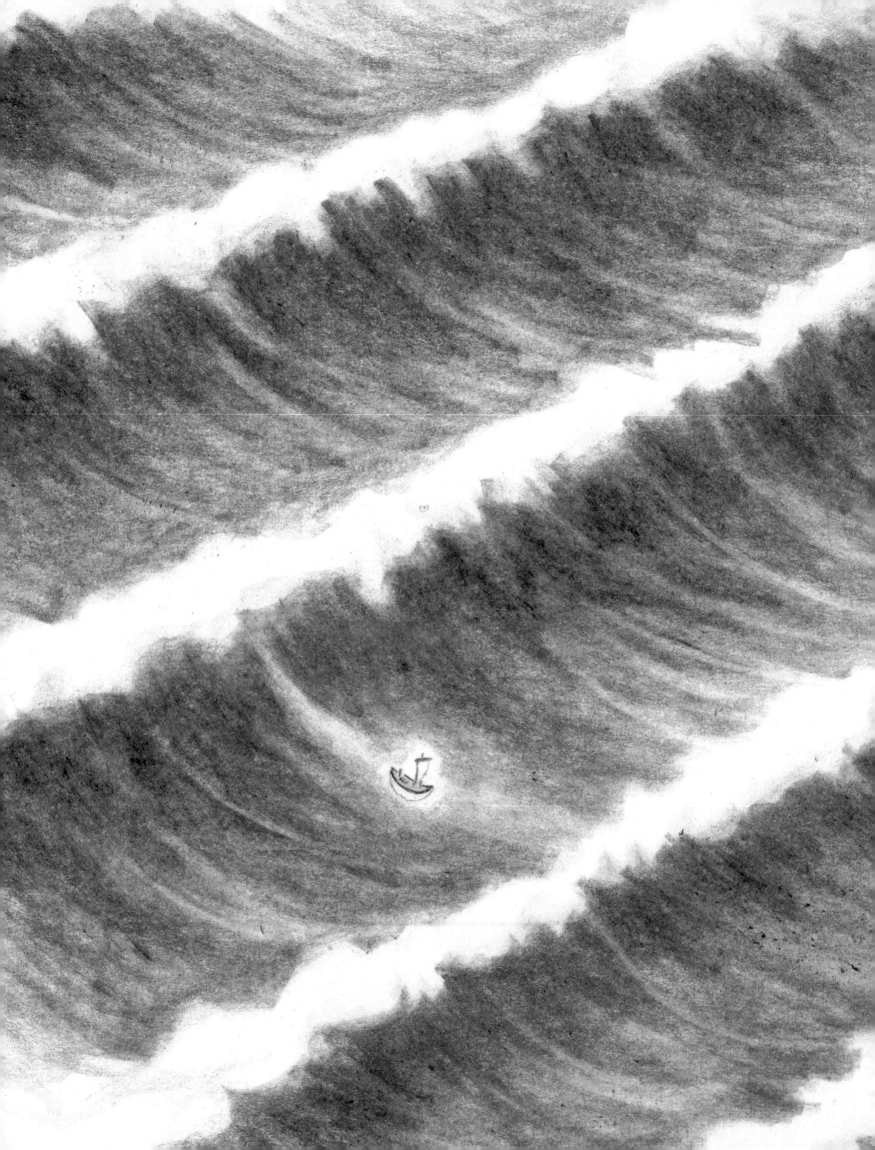

MEANWHILE ON ELEPHANT ISLAND

Bad weather had settled in, and 30-foot waves crashed down onto the beach, threatening to wash away the camp.

To combat the violent weather, Marston (the artist) had the ingenious idea to turn the boats upside down and convert them into shelters, allowing his oil paints to be used as glue so that canvas sheets could be fixed to the boats for extra waterproofing.

Little adjustments were gradually made to the camp to make life more bearable – they added chimneys in the roofs, raised the shelters higher and carved a gutter in the ground to avoid getting wet.

Food was now running very low and the men were weak. Wild, always the optimist, proved to be a guiding light, making the men laugh as well as settling any disturbances – such as the time when Orde-Lees challenged Macklin to a duel on the beach at dawn, with broken oars as weapons!

Wild knew that if the men sat about doing nothing they would start to deteriorate further, so he kept them busy with various jobs, giving them each a purpose and responsibility.

Another calming influence on the party was Hussey's cheerful banjo playing, and the party would look forward to concerts every Saturday. Small treats like these made a huge difference to the men, and were key to keeping them sane while they waited for rescue.

MAP OF SOUTH GEORGIA

MORRIS GLACIER

PURVIS GLACIER

PEGGOTTY CAMP

CREAN GLACIER

MURRAY SNOWFIELD

ESMARK GLACIER

After battling monstrous waves and ferocious winds for ten days straight, Shackleton's party arrived happily at King Haakon Bay, South Georgia. However, their gruelling journey was not over yet. They sailed the little boat along the coast until they found a suitable spot to land. Their first thought being shelter, they took refuge and recuperated in a small cave, guarded by 15-foot-long icicles.

FORTUNA GLACIER

STROMNESS

CREVASSES

WILCKENS
PEAKS

NEUMAYER GLACIER

Shackleton knew it was now time to venture across the island to
seek help at the Stromness whaling station. The whalers themselves
thought the interior of the island to be impenetrable. But Shackleton
realised that the quickest route would be overland, so he moved
down towards the head of the bay and established Peggotty Camp,
creating a shelter from the upturned boat.

He decided to cross the island with Crean and Worsley, leaving
the other three men behind and taking enough provisions for
three days. Crean had experience in alpine environments, and
Worsley was an experienced mountaineer and had proved himself a
splendid navigator.

CROSSING SOUTH GEORGIA

✳

On their trek, the three men encountered unknown mountains shrouded in loose rock and ice, fields of thick snow, **gullies**, deep **crevasses** and jigsaw-like **glaciers**. As well as overcoming such obstacles, they had to battle altitude sickness, **dehydration**, immense hunger and exhaustion. They were now reaching their limit.

STROMNESS WHALING STATION

The men had now been moving non-stop for over 36 hours. Then, in the distance, the vague shape of Husvik harbour emerged like a beacon of hope. Upon sighting the harbour, the men shook hands with one another in silence.

All that separated the men from their sanctuary was a huge snow slope that seemed to end in a **precipice**. It was either this route or a five-mile walk to get around the drop. Without too much thought, they went for it, crashing and sliding down together. Their clothes shredded, and stripped of all their belongings, they had arrived.

The manager of the station, Mr Sorlle, came out to see what the fuss was about, but did not recognise the exhausted, broken men in front of him until one of them explained, "My name is Shackleton." Then Sorlle immediately reached out to the men and took them inside.

Sorlle was a most gracious host, and saw to it that the men had plenty of food, drink and hot water to bathe. A boat was sent to King Haakon Bay to pick up the three men who had been left behind. Once they had recovered, the men all sat together and discussed immediate plans to rescue their friends on Elephant Island. To save them, Shackleton would need a vessel strong enough to break through the pack ice, with enough fuel to return to land. Luckily, the Chilean government lent Shackleton a steam-powered ship called the Yelcho.

RESCUE

Finally, on 30 August 1916, help arrived for the men on Elephant Island after three failed attempts to reach the island due to heavy ice. The moment that the rescuers spotted the camp, the men on the island rushed to the shore, frantically waving and calling in joy. Shackleton shouted, "Are you all well?" and Wild answered, "We are all well, Boss," followed by the cheers of the whole crew. Shackleton had arrived just in time, as the men were weak and frail. By a miracle, Wild had kept hope alive.

DEPARTURE

Worried about being trapped by the ice, Shackleton had his men hastily rushed aboard, fired the little steamer's engines and headed north for South America. The men all agreed that they would honour and remember 30 August for the rest of their lives.

Exhausted and glad to be alive, the crew steamed away on the Yelcho while Wild recalled stories of their life waiting on the island. The men would later receive a hero's welcome in Punta Arenas, Chile, where 30,000 people filled the streets warmly awaiting their return.

Against all the odds, Shackleton had ended his expedition without losing a single member of Endurance's crew.

THE ROSS SEA PARTY

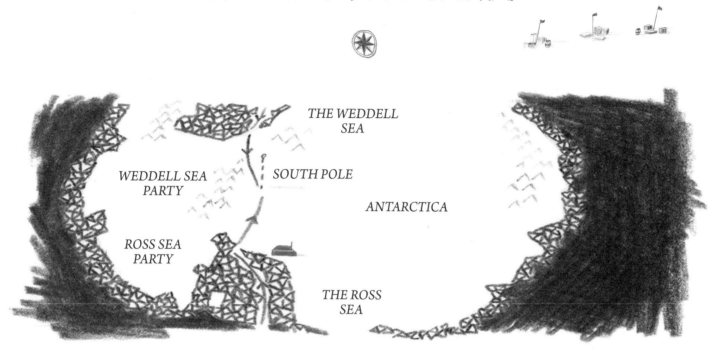

While Shackleton and his crew were approaching Antarctica from the Weddell Sea, the support team for the Endurance mission were undertaking an equally perilous journey. Although the details of the Ross Sea Party have historically been less documented, their task was no less ambitious and physically challenging.

Shackleton's plan was for the crew of the Aurora to leave stores of food at regular intervals from the Ross Sea coast to a calculated distance inland. At a good walking pace, Shackleton and his men would just be able to make it to the first of the **depots** set up by the Ross Sea Party.

The Ross Sea party formed the second part of the Endurance mission to cross Antarctica on foot. While Shackleton and his crew approached Antarctica from the Weddell Sea, the Ross Sea Party (captained by Aeneas Mackintosh) would be approaching from the other side to support Shackleton's march overland.

Arriving in the Ross Sea in early 1914, Captain Mackintosh and the crew of the Aurora quickly set about their task, loading supplies onto dog sledges and striking inland. But conditions were against them – heavy snowfalls and terrible weather meant that progress was slow and difficult.

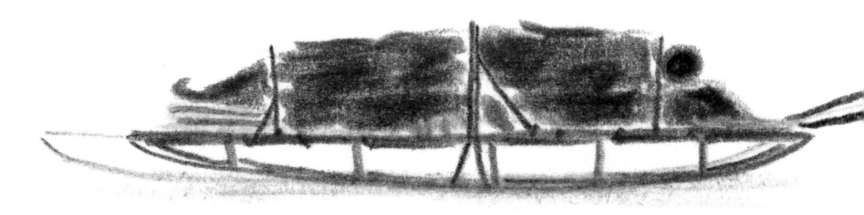

Then, after months of hardship on the ice, disaster struck: in May 1915, the Aurora was swept away during a storm and found herself trapped in the pack ice, unable to return. As the damaged ship slowly drifted towards New Zealand, the ten men who were left behind were now the only humans on the whole continent.

But conditions were taking their toll – with dogs, supplies and energy running low, the stranded men suffered from **scurvy**, frostbite and exhaustion.

These brave souls had no way of knowing that the Endurance was also stranded in the ice on the other side of Antarctica, and that Shackleton and his explorers had never even begun their long march overland. Sticking to the original plan, the Aurora team battled to complete their mission over the next year, laying down the depots as instructed for Shackleton and his crew.

Despite their heroic group effort, Mackintosh and Hayward were lost on the sea ice, while Spencer-Smith, the chaplain, eventually died from scurvy.

Following Shackleton's epic journey to save the crew of the Endurance, he then rushed to New Zealand to oversee efforts to reach the remaining members of the Ross Sea Party. Finally, in January 1917, rescue arrived.

The expedition to cross Antarctica had failed, but the majority of both crews had survived through an extraordinary combination of bravery, strength of character and endurance.

HOME AT LAST

In memory of all the brave men and dogs who ventured south on
Shackleton's journey.

"I chose life over death for myself and my friends...
I believe it is in our nature to explore, to reach out into the
unknown. The only true failure would be to not explore at all."

– Ernest Shackleton

GLOSSARY

ANTARCTICA
The most southerly continent on Earth, covered in snow and ice.

BLIZZARD
A heavy snowstorm.

BLUBBER
Animal fat, used as both food and fuel.

CAPSIZE
When a boat is overturned in water.

COMPASS
A magnetic instrument showing north, used in navigation.

CONNING
Directing the steering of a ship.

CREVASSE
A deep crack in ice.

CROSS-BRACING
A system of wooden beams which adds strength to a structure.

CROW'S NEST
A platform at the top of a ship's mast.

DEHYDRATION
The loss of water from the body, especially from illness or physical exertion.

DEPOT
A place where supplies are stored.

FLOE
A sheet of floating ice.

FORESAIL
The sail at the front of a ship.

FROSTBITE
An injury caused by exposure to extreme cold.

GALE
A very strong wind.

GLACIER
A huge mass of ice and snow, often moving very slowly down from a mountain top.

WINTER MONTHS
Due to the tilt of the Earth's axis, the Northern and Southern Hemispheres experience the seasons at different times. In the Southern Hemisphere, Midwinter's Day takes place in June.

GROWLER
A block of ice large enough to damage a ship, often floating underwater.

GULLY
A small valley caused by rain and running water.

HULL
The main body of a ship.

HUMMOCK
Where forces of nature and weather have heaved ice into a mound.

IGLOO
A dome-shaped hut made from hard snow.

JIB BOOM
A wooden extension at the front of a ship.

KENNEL
A shelter for dogs.

PACK ICE
A large area of ice formed when many smaller pieces of ice are pushed together by the sea or the wind.

PRECIPICE
A cliff with a vertical face.

PRESSURE RIDGE
A hump formed in floating ice by crushing pressure.

RATIONS
Fixed daily amounts of food.

REEFING A SAIL
Reducing the size of a sail.

SCURVY
A disease caused by lack of vitamin C.

SEA LEOPARD
A large and ferocious type of seal, sometimes called a leopard seal.

SLEDGE
A vehicle, sometimes pulled by dogs, used for transport over ice and snow.

SOUTH POLE
The most southerly point on Earth.

MIX
Paper from
responsible sources
FSC® C101807

This is a fifth edition.

Shackleton's Journey is © 2014 Flying Eye Books.
All artwork and text within are © 2014 William Grill.
Written by William Grill. Edited by Dan Lockwood.

Published by Flying Eye Books, an imprint of Nobrow Ltd.
62 Great Eastern Street, London, EC2A 3QR.

Published in the US by Flying Eye Books, an imprint of Nobrow (US) Inc.,
611 Broadway, Suite #742, NY 10012, New York, USA

ISBN 978-1-909263-10-9
Printed in Belgium on FSC assured paper

Order from www.flyingeyebooks.com